The Test o

Contents

Bright Ideas	4
Changes in Inventions	
Over the Millennia	6
Over the Centuries	8
Over the Decades	10
An Inventive World	12
Eureka!	14
Before Their Time	15
Entertaining Inventions	20
Taking a Closer Look	22
Young Inventors	24
Naming Thingamajigs	26
The Real McCoy	28
Glossary	30
Index	31
Research Starters	32

Features

TIME LINK

Discover how clocks, aircraft and computers have changed over time. Follow the time lines on pages 6–11.

FACT FINDER

Solve the riddles in **An Inventive World** on page 12 and discover the origins of seven inventions.

IN FOCUS

What could popcorn and a hairdryer have in common? Read **Young Inventors** on page 24 to find out.

WORD BUILDER

How do inventors decide what to call a new invention? Find out in **Naming Thingamajigs** on page 26.

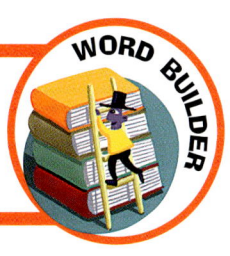

SITESEEING · SCIENCE & TECHNOLOGY

How can a rocket fly without fuel?
Visit **www.infosteps.co.uk** for more about **SPACE TECHNOLOGY**.

Bright Ideas

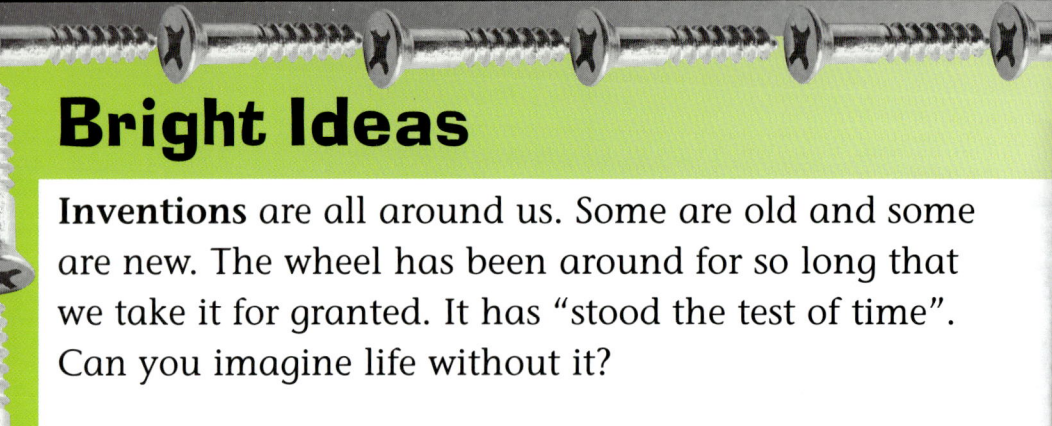

Inventions are all around us. Some are old and some are new. The wheel has been around for so long that we take it for granted. It has "stood the test of time". Can you imagine life without it?

Other inventions did not stand the test of time. **Zeppelin** airships were popular for only thirty years until a disaster made people stop using them. Horse-drawn carriages stood the test of time for many centuries, but the motor car quickly replaced them. Carriage makers and other people lost their jobs. Many new jobs, however, were created by the automobile industry.

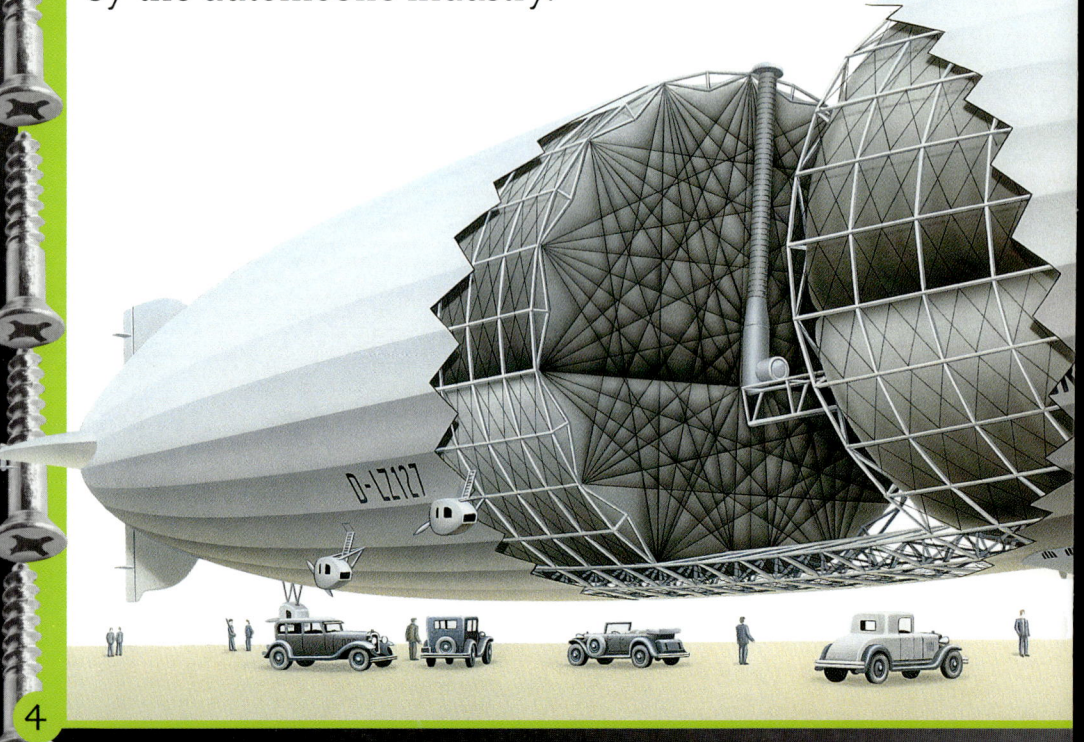

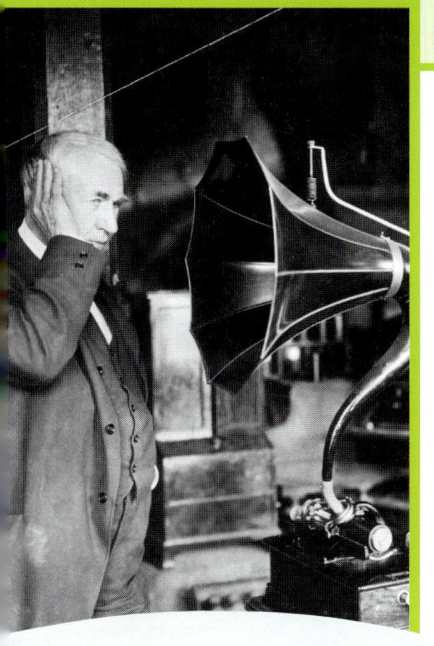

Did You Know?

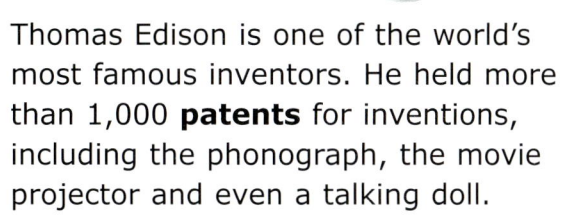

Thomas Edison is one of the world's most famous inventors. He held more than 1,000 **patents** for inventions, including the phonograph, the movie projector and even a talking doll.

Edison made the first practical light bulb and had the bright idea of lighting up New York City. Now when we draw someone having a bright idea we often put a light bulb above them!

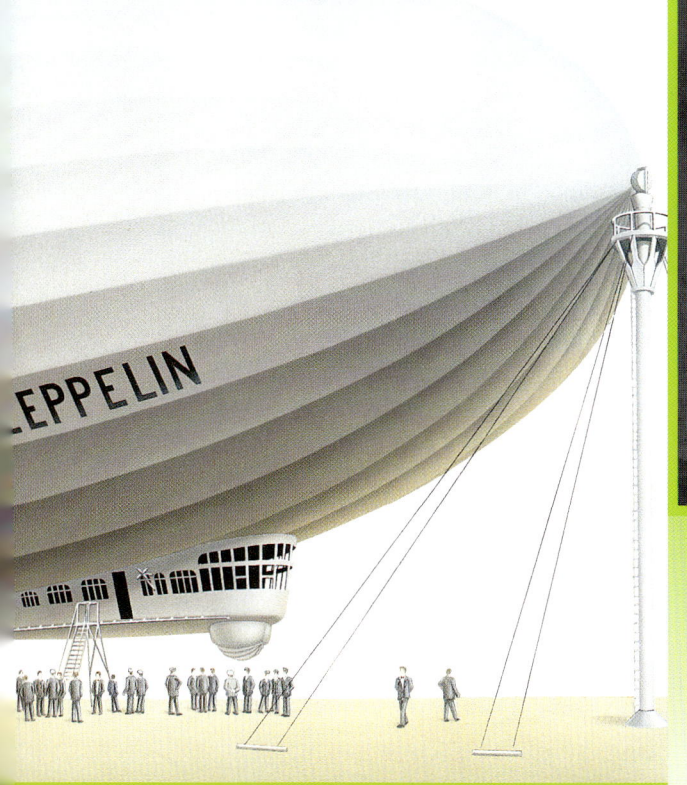

Travel by airships was no longer popular after the *Hindenburg* Zeppelin burst into flames while landing in 1937.

Changes in Inventions

Over the Millennia

Many inventions have been around for **millennia**. The ancient Chinese invented the compass, the umbrella and chopsticks. The first metal coins and paper money also came from China.

Many inventions today are improvements on inventions that have been around for a long time. Soap, for example, was invented 4,000 years ago, but it was very expensive. Scientific discoveries in the 1800s led to cheaper ways of making soap.

TIME LINK Inventions to measure time are more than 3,000 years old!

The water clock was invented in Egypt over 3,000 years ago. It was used to tell how much time had passed during a day.

The hourglass was invented about 1,300 years ago. It uses fine sand to measure small amounts of time.

The first mechanical clock in Europe was built around 1300. This clock wasn't very precise.

Muscle-Powered Machines

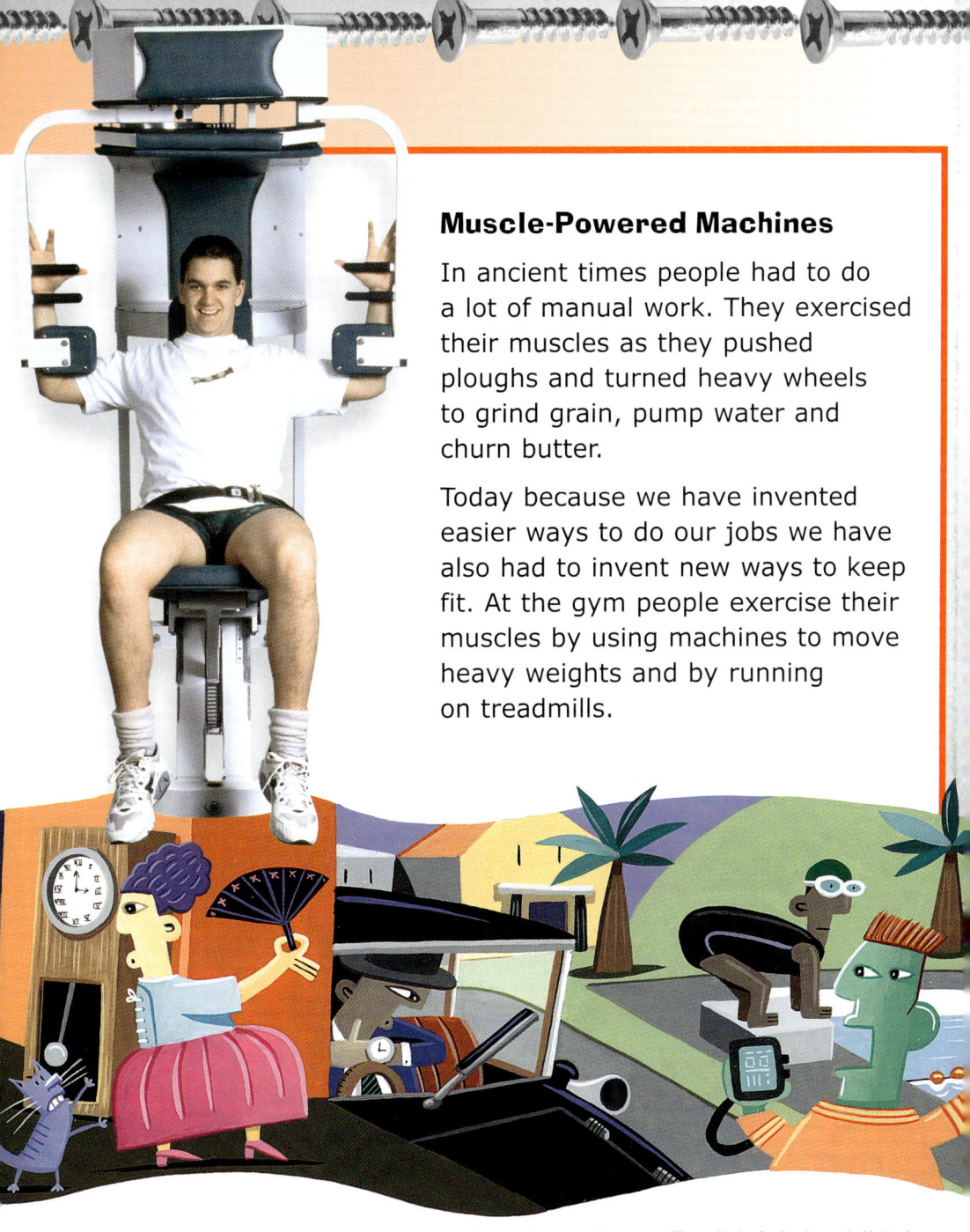

In ancient times people had to do a lot of manual work. They exercised their muscles as they pushed ploughs and turned heavy wheels to grind grain, pump water and churn butter.

Today because we have invented easier ways to do our jobs we have also had to invent new ways to keep fit. At the gym people exercise their muscles by using machines to move heavy weights and by running on treadmills.

The pendulum clock was invented in 1656. The pendulum helped keep correct time.

The wristwatch was invented in 1907. It became popular during World War I.

The digital clock and digital watch became popular inventions in the 1970s.

Over the Centuries

Some inventions have been around for hundreds of years. Many of these came from Europe, including the mirror (600 years old), the printing press (500 years old) and the flush toilet (400 years old).

Several models for steam engines were designed before James Watt of Scotland invented the first practical steam engine in 1769. This invention was the most important machine made during the **Industrial Revolution**. New uses for the steam engine were quickly found, bringing many changes to industry and transportation.

Inventive minds have brought many changes to air travel.

In 1783 two Frenchmen were the first human passengers in a hot-air balloon.

In the 1800s Otto Lilienthal of Germany built the first glider that could carry a person.

In 1903 the Wright brothers, of the United States, made the first aeroplane flight with a petrol engine.

Changes in Inventions continued

The first steam locomotive was invented in the early 1800s. Steam continued to power many trains for more than a century.

In 1939 Russian-born Igor Sikorsky designed and flew the first useful helicopter.

In 1949 the first jet-engine airliner was invented. It travelled at 782 kilometres per hour.

In 1969 the Concorde, the first commercial supersonic plane, made its first flight.

9

Over the Decades

Some inventions have been around for less than a century and have followed the increasing use of electricity in homes. **Mass production** has made many inventions more reliable and less costly. These inventions include the television (1929), the microwave oven (1946), CDs (compact discs, 1982) and DVDs (digital versatile discs, 1994).

Inventions in recent decades have changed rapidly. When the **laser** was invented in 1960 it had little use. Now lasers are used in CD players, medical surgery, supermarket scanners and earthquake sensors.

Computers have changed a great deal over the decades.

The first electronic digital computer was invented in the 1940s. It was so large that it filled most of a building.

The silicon chip was invented in 1959. This allowed computers to become faster and smaller.

The personal computer (PC) was developed in 1975 in the United States.

Changes in Inventions continued

Lasers are used for research in many areas of science.

In 1987 a laptop computer weighing less than a kilogram was invented in England.

Today computers are common in many homes. They can be both educational and entertaining.

In the future robots with computers for "brains" may become a common sight.

11

An Inventive World

FACT FINDER

Canada

Netherlands

United States

Answers:
D3 – Chess
A2 – Television
E2 – Umbrella
C2 – Telescope
F4 – Bungee jump
B2 – Paint roller
E4 – Boomerang

Inventions come from many different countries. Solve these riddles to find seven inventions and where they came from.

- **D3** This game of strategy is played on different coloured squares.
- **A2** Some people say too much of this will give you square eyes.
- **E2** This keeps you dry and shaded.
- **C2** Things look larger when you look at them through this tube.
- **F4** In this activity people jump from high places with a cord tied to their ankles.
- **B2** People use this instead of a paintbrush.
- **E4** Throw this away and it comes right back to you.

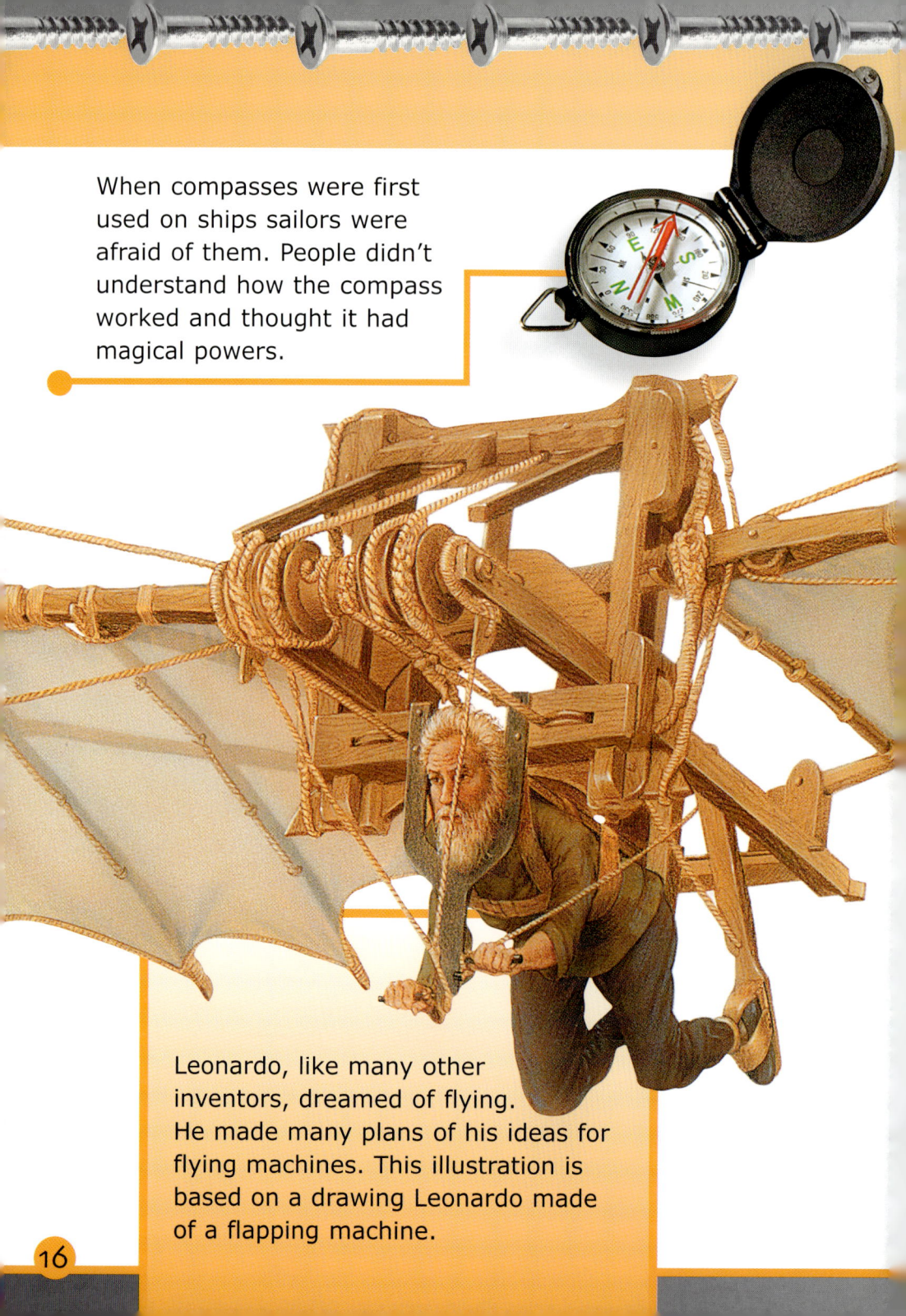

When compasses were first used on ships sailors were afraid of them. People didn't understand how the compass worked and thought it had magical powers.

Leonardo, like many other inventors, dreamed of flying. He made many plans of his ideas for flying machines. This illustration is based on a drawing Leonardo made of a flapping machine.

Before Their Time

Leonardo da Vinci was the first person to scientifically study the flight of birds. Leonardo was born in Italy over 500 years ago during a time called the **Renaissance**. He was a great artist, architect and thinker. Leonardo drew plans for tools, weapons and machines. Many of his designs still look modern today.

Most of Leonardo's ideas, however, were ahead of their time and too difficult for the people of the day to build. With improved technology many of his ideas have been "re-invented".

Today someone who is very inventive and knowledgeable, especially in both art and science, may be called "a Renaissance person".

Eureka!

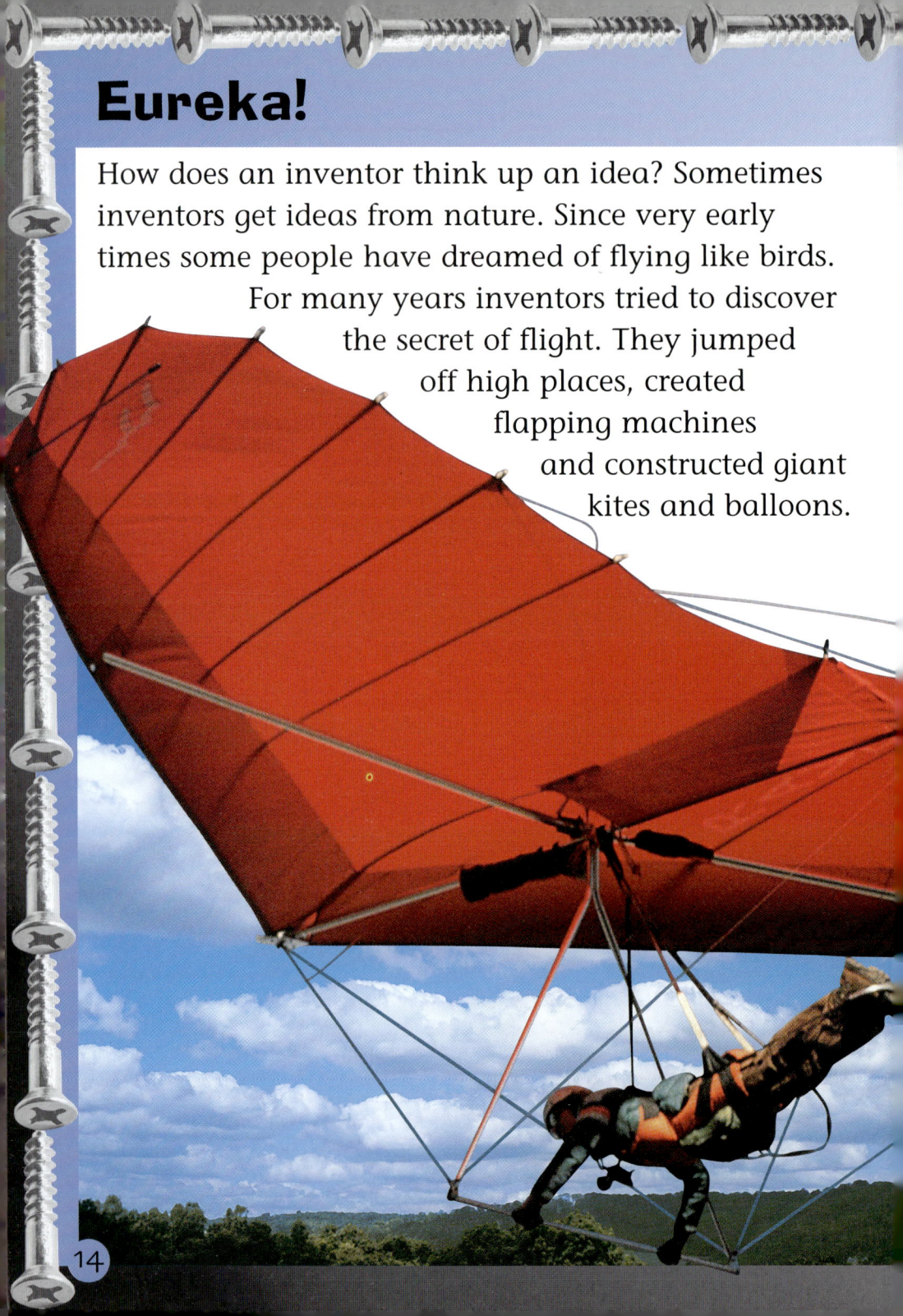

How does an inventor think up an idea? Sometimes inventors get ideas from nature. Since very early times some people have dreamed of flying like birds. For many years inventors tried to discover the secret of flight. They jumped off high places, created flapping machines and constructed giant kites and balloons.

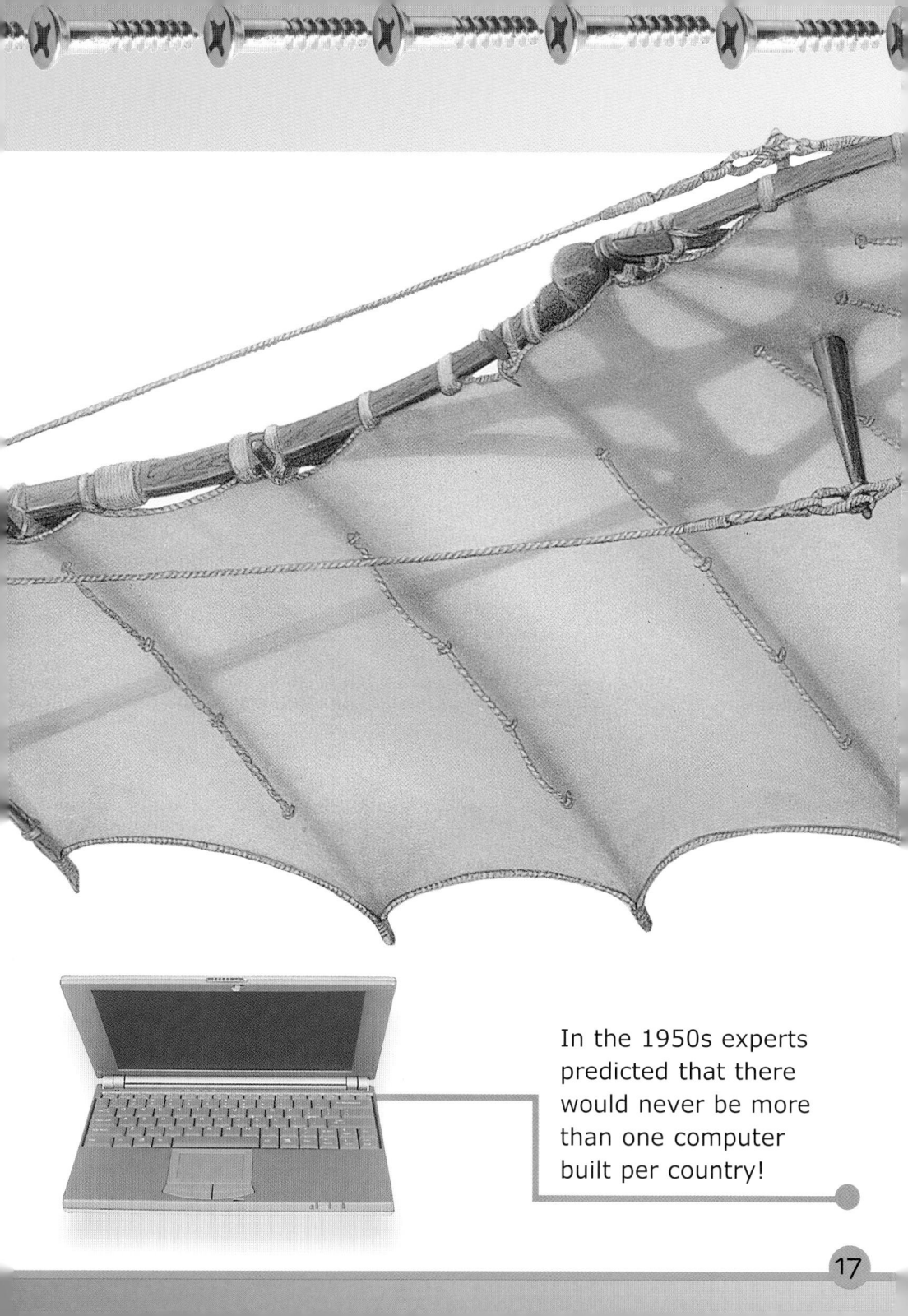

In the 1950s experts predicted that there would never be more than one computer built per country!

Entertaining Inventions

The piano was invented in Italy in 1709 by Bartolommeo Cristofori. Pianos soon became very popular around the world and they were often the main form of family entertainment.

The invention of the radio in 1895 by another Italian, Guglielmo Marconi, led to great changes in the everyday lives of many people. By the 1920s radio stations in many countries brought entertainment and news into people's homes.

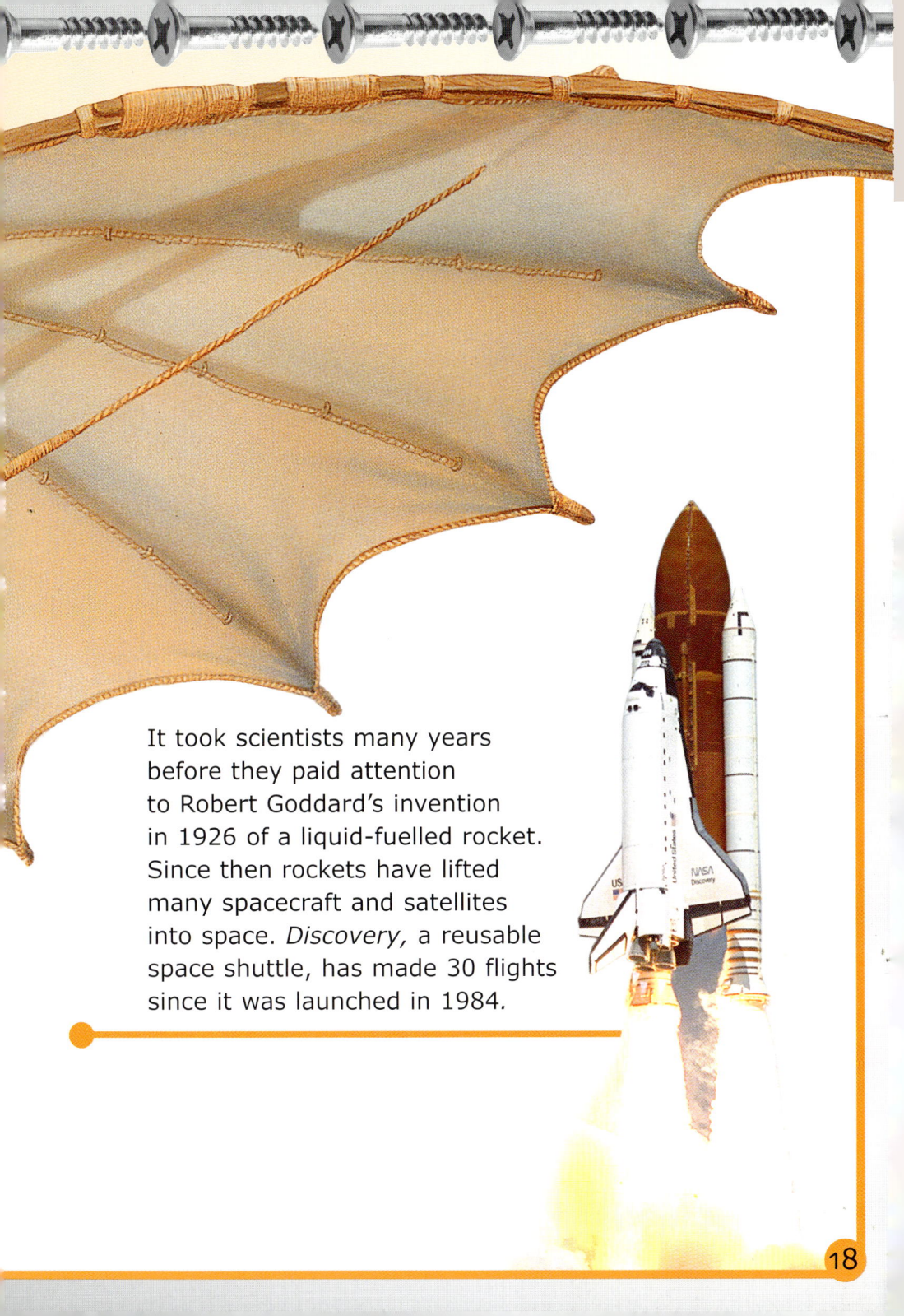

It took scientists many years before they paid attention to Robert Goddard's invention in 1926 of a liquid-fuelled rocket. Since then rockets have lifted many spacecraft and satellites into space. *Discovery,* a reusable space shuttle, has made 30 flights since it was launched in 1984.

WORD BUILDER

Archimedes was an inventor and mathematician who lived in ancient Greece. When he suddenly thought of a way to determine the purity of gold he jumped up shouting *Heuraka!*—Greek for "I have found it!" Today people often shout *eureka* when they are excited about a new discovery.

The invention of the hang-glider developed from research at NASA in the 1940s and 1950s. Hang-gliding became a popular sport in the early 1970s.

Thomas Edison invented the first practical **phonograph** in 1877. It was the most common device for listening to recorded music until the mid-1980s when cassette tapes and CDs became more common. Today people can watch live world events on television and they can play computer games with friends.

Taking a Closer Look

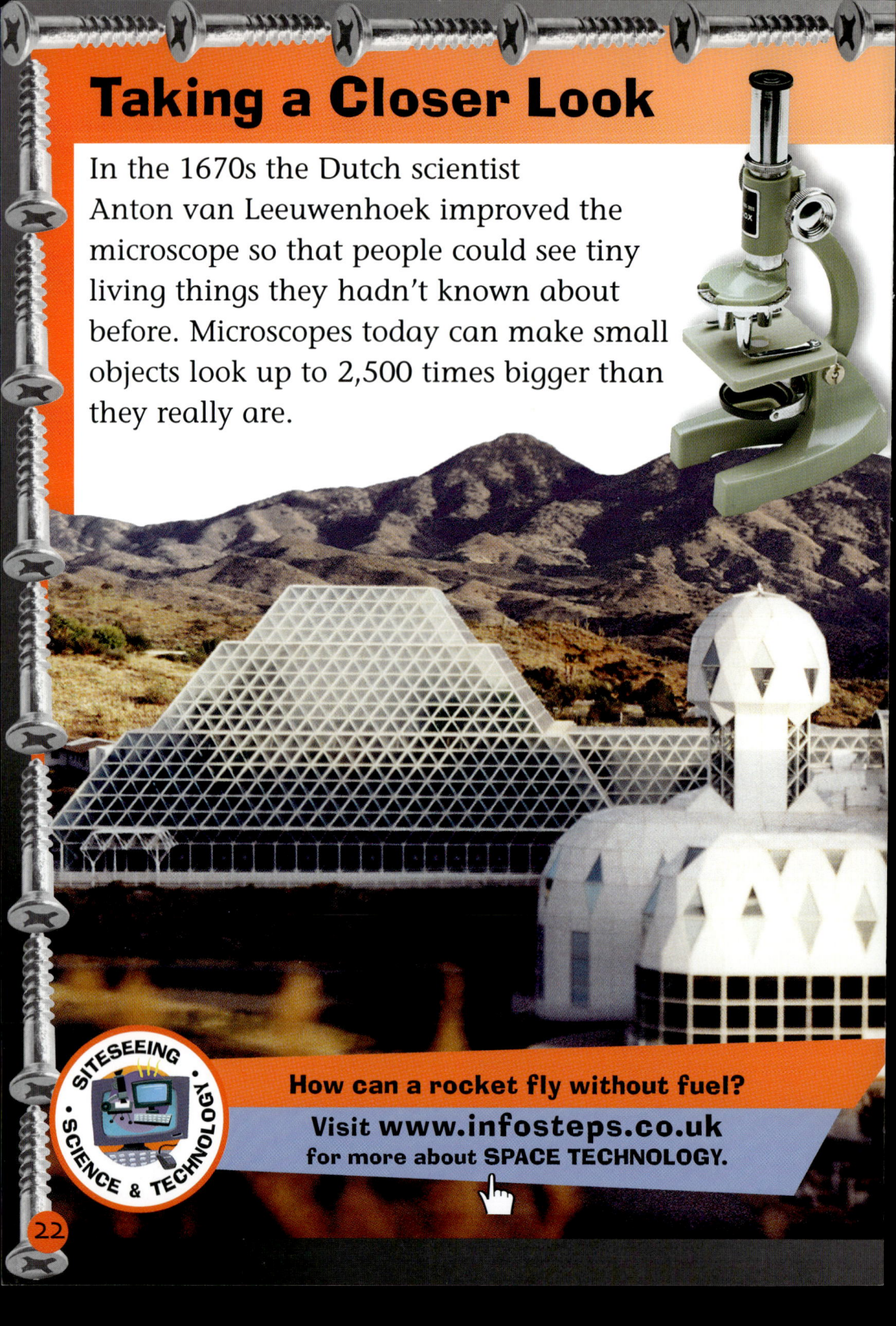

In the 1670s the Dutch scientist Anton van Leeuwenhoek improved the microscope so that people could see tiny living things they hadn't known about before. Microscopes today can make small objects look up to 2,500 times bigger than they really are.

How can a rocket fly without fuel?

Visit **www.infosteps.co.uk**
for more about **SPACE TECHNOLOGY**.

Other inventions help people to explore Earth and space. The invention of the first deep-ocean submersibles in the 1930s allowed people to study sea life in its natural habitat. Today people can live in space for short periods of time in space stations to perform experiments and test new inventions.

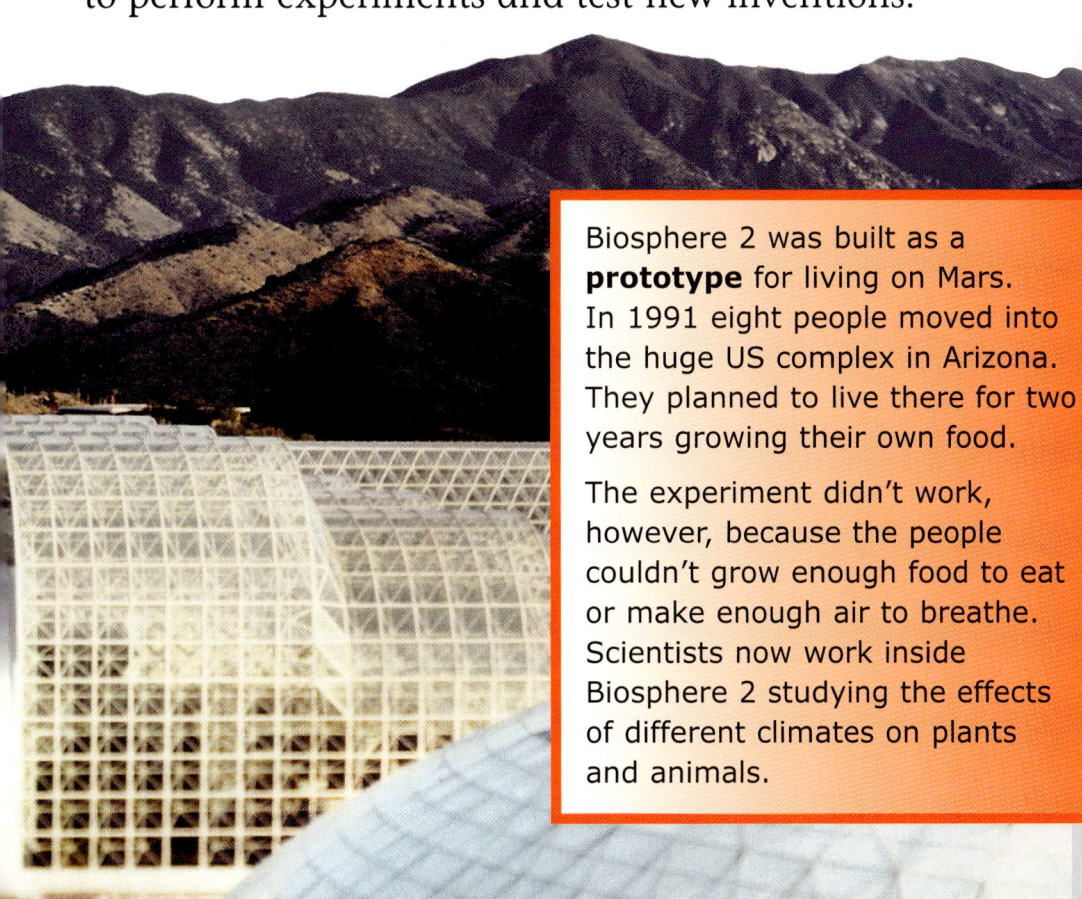

Biosphere 2 was built as a **prototype** for living on Mars. In 1991 eight people moved into the huge US complex in Arizona. They planned to live there for two years growing their own food.

The experiment didn't work, however, because the people couldn't grow enough food to eat or make enough air to breathe. Scientists now work inside Biosphere 2 studying the effects of different climates on plants and animals.

IN FOCUS

Young Inventors

Students have the chance to show their inventive ideas at school science fairs and competitions. The students' experiments and inventions often come about from thinking of possible solutions to problems.

Science and technology museums are exciting places to learn about inventions and how things work. Displays are designed so that visitors can discover for themselves the secrets behind inventions.

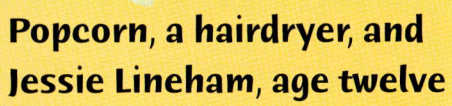

Popcorn, a hairdryer, and Jessie Lineham, age twelve

Jessie was given a hairdryer for her birthday. There was one problem: "It was so noisy it made my ears ring."

The Noisy Challenge
Jessie, a previous regional finalist in a national science and technology competition, decided making the hairdryer quiet would be her next challenge. She spent over one year on the project. "The hardest part was testing my ideas over and over again."

A Good Hair Day
Finally Jessie came up with a solution—a clip-on plastic tube containing popcorn that reduces the noise of the hairdryer's motor. Jessie's clever invention was displayed at the national science and technology fair. Jessie adds, "I can now dry my hair without hurting my ears."

WORD BUILDER

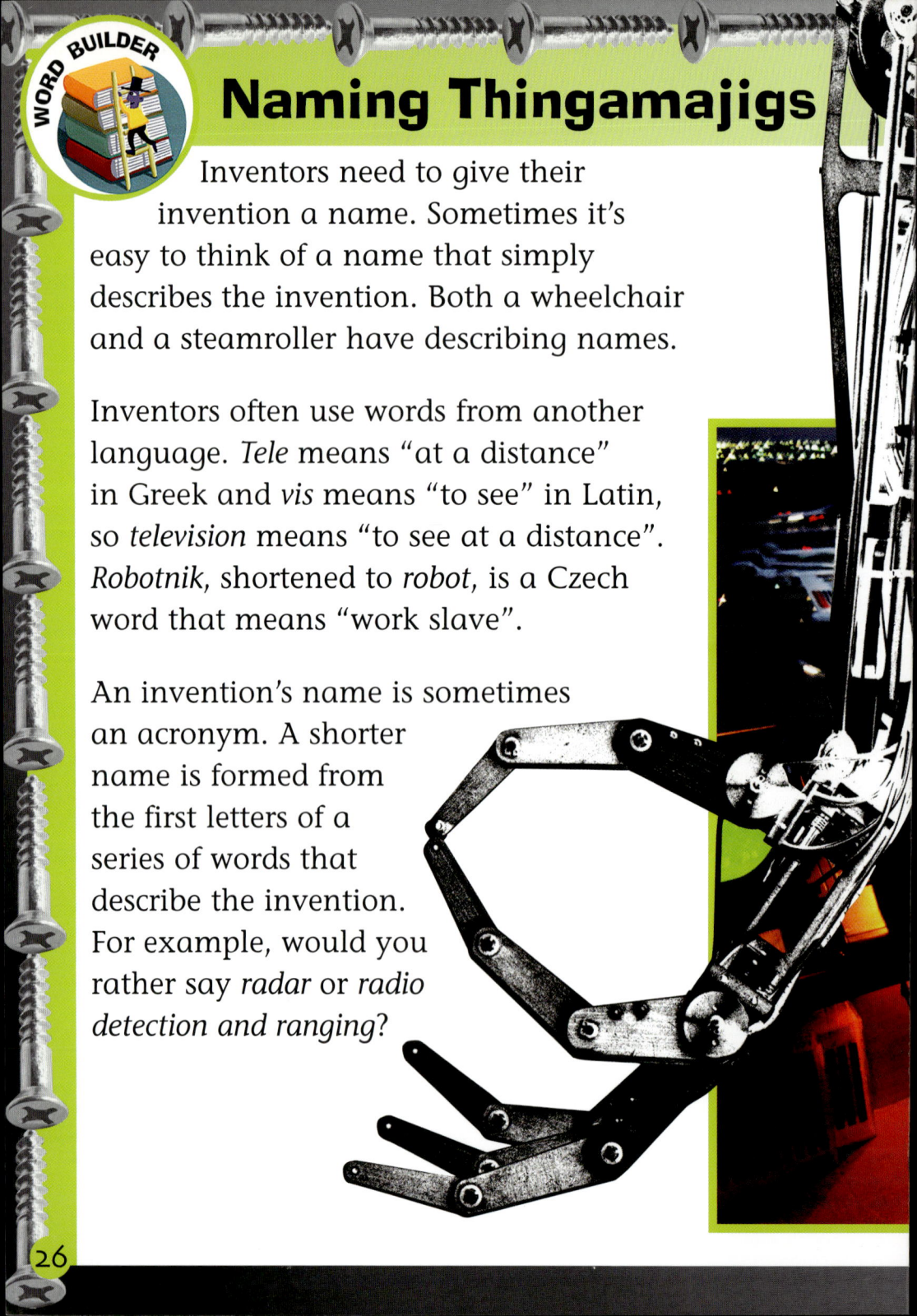

Naming Thingamajigs

Inventors need to give their invention a name. Sometimes it's easy to think of a name that simply describes the invention. Both a wheelchair and a steamroller have describing names.

Inventors often use words from another language. *Tele* means "at a distance" in Greek and *vis* means "to see" in Latin, so *television* means "to see at a distance". *Robotnik*, shortened to *robot*, is a Czech word that means "work slave".

An invention's name is sometimes an acronym. A shorter name is formed from the first letters of a series of words that describe the invention. For example, would you rather say *radar* or *radio detection and ranging*?

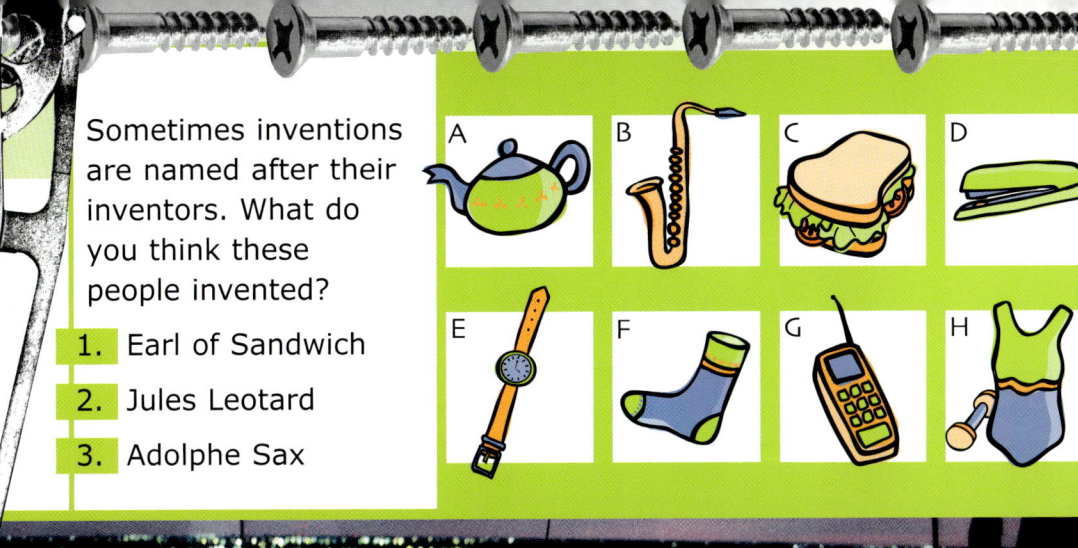

Sometimes inventions are named after their inventors. What do you think these people invented?

1. Earl of Sandwich
2. Jules Leotard
3. Adolphe Sax

Radar

Radar uses radio waves to locate aircraft in the sky.

Answers: 1. C, sandwich 2. H, leotard 3. B, saxophone

27

The Real McCoy

Have you ever heard the expression "the real McCoy"? It is used when people want to make sure they are getting the best or the genuine item instead of a copy. Inventors patent their ideas to protect their inventions from being copied and so people can be sure they get the genuine item.

In the last 500 years, over 25 million patents have been taken out—and people continue inventing new things. In 1890 the US Commissioner of Patents wondered if he should retire because he thought everything useful had already been invented!

WORD BUILDER

McCoy was in fact a real person. Elijah McCoy was born in 1843 in Ontario, Canada. He was the son of African American slaves who had escaped from Kentucky before the Civil War.

While working on the railways McCoy invented and patented a machine that would oil steam engines. This machine worked far better than any other device, though many people tried to copy McCoy's idea. Owners insisted, however, that the "real McCoy" be in their engines.

Nappy alarm

Remote-control mop

Car sun shield

Wacky Inventions
Here are some unusual inventions that people have patented!

Combination trumpet and flame-thrower

Motorized ice-cream cone

Swinging-arm device for doing a high five

29

Glossary

Industrial Revolution – a time when many important inventions were made, bringing great change to the lives of many people. The Revolution began in Britain in the 1700s and had spread through Europe and North America by the mid–1800s.

invention – a new device, method or process developed in experiments

laser – a device that makes a very narrow and powerful beam of light. A laser can be used for very fine work such as cutting things or guiding machines.

mass production – the method of making large numbers of identical items, usually by machinery in a factory

millennia – thousands of years. A millennium is a period of one thousand years.

patent – an agreement made between an inventor and a government. A patent gives only the inventor the right to make and sell the invention for a set amount of time.

phonograph – a machine that plays records. Records have grooves in which sounds have been recorded.

prototype – an early model of an invention. The prototype tests an idea to see if it will work.

Renaissance – a period of time in Europe between the 1300s and 1500s. The Renaissance was a time of renewed interest in the arts and learning.

Zeppelin – a long airship that is filled with a lighter-than-air gas

Index

aircraft	4–5, 8–9
Biosphere 2	22–23
clocks	6–7
computers	10–11, 17, 21
hang-gliders	14, 19
inventors	
Archimedes	19
Cristofori, Bartolommeo	20
Edison, Thomas	5, 21
Goddard, Robert	18
Leeuwenhoek, Anton van	22
Lineham, Jessie	25
McCoy, Elijah	28
Marconi, Guglielmo	20
Vinci, Leonardo da	15–18
Watt, James	8
lasers	10–11
microscopes	22
patents	5, 28–29
pianos	20
radar	26–27
robots	11, 26
steam engines	8–9
televisions	10, 12, 26

Research Starters

1 Thomas Edison patented more than 1,000 inventions. Find out about some of his inventions and write a description of what you think life might be like without them. Edison once said that "genius is 1% inspiration and 99% perspiration". What do you think he meant?

2 In **An Inventive World** on pages 12–13 eight inventions haven't been labelled. Find them and then research the history of one of these inventions.

3 The invention of the car has dramatically changed our lives. Today there are more than 400 million cars on roads around the world. What do you think have been the advantages and disadvantages of this invention?

4 Imagine you have invented a device that lets people smell something at a distance in the same way a telephone or radio lets you hear things at a distance. Think of an acronym for your invention.